101 Ways to Know. . .You're a Golddigger

Also by the Wayans Brothers

101 Ways to Know It's Time to Leave Your Mama's House
101 Ways to Know You're Having a Ghetto Christmas

101

ways to know . . .

You're a Golddigger

Keenen Ivory Wayans,
Shawn Wayans,
and Marlon Wayans

St. Martin's Griffin 🐾 New York

www.stmartins.com

Library of Congress Cataloging-in-Publication Data

Wayans, Keenen Ivory.
   101 ways to know you're a golddigger/keenen, Shawn, and Marlon Wayans.—1st ed.
          p. cm.
    ISBN-13: 978-0-312-35969-0
    ISBN-10: 0-312-35969-1
   1. Women—Humor. 2. Invective—Humor. I. Wayans, Shawn, 1971–II. Wayans, Marlon. III. Title.
    PN6231.W68A35 2009
    818'.5402—dc22

                                                              2009004805

First Edition: May 2009

10 9 8 7 6 5 4 3 2 1

Acknowledgments

Thank you to our family, all 9 million of them, and to our team:
Rick Alvarez, Lisa Bloom, Mike Tiddes, Luom Cooper, Coral
Compagnoni, and Danielle Casinelli.
Special thanks to Shane Miller, Darren Huang,
Layron Dejarnette, and David Torres.
Thank you all for your contributions.

101 Ways to Know. . .You're a Golddigger

You know you're a golddigger if . . .

Super-Head is your role model.

You date a celebrity's whole entourage, just to get close to the celebrity.

You know more about a sports players' stats than ESPN analysts.

You name your kids after all the expensive gifts you hope to attain . . . Porsche, Mercedes, Diamond, A-lexus, Money.

You stay in an abusive relationship for the nice gifts he gives you.

You're only twenty-one and you claim you married an
eighty-year-old oil tycoon for love.

Your lifelong ambition is to be one of Hugh Hefner's wives.

You refer to your marriage as "a smart business move."

You have kids who look like you but sound like the nanny.

The only time you cried during your divorce was when
you were awarded your settlement.

You tell your millionaire fiancé that a prenuptial agreement
will jinx the marriage.

You asked your husband for a diamond ring bigger than your head .

You divorce your rich husband but keep his last name to get into clubs.

You get divorced but use the kids' child support money for lavish trips and shopping sprees.

You have floor seats at the Lakers game but you work at the GAP.

Kanye West's "Gold Digger" is your anthem.

Your top eight on MySpace are all celebrities you don't know but hope to sleep with.

You think there's "something sexy" about . . .
1. Hugh Hefner   2. Flavor Flav   3. Sam Cassell

You are in the VIP area of a club but never bought a bottle.

You slept with a guy hoping he'd pay to get your cavity fixed.

Your boyfriend's father has more money, so you dump him for his daddy.

You marry a rich man even though his kids don't like you.

You were on *Flavor of Love.*

You made your first million in your first marriage, your second million in your second marriage, and you retired in your third marriage.

You changed your faith to conform to your rich husband's beliefs.

CONTRACT

This contract states that ___BJ___ agrees that she will perform sex for the amount of one million U.S. dollars. Payment shall be payed in full on completion of sexual acts or favors. Any added requests after the initial agreement is negotiable.

Bonita Jenkins ♡
Bonita Jenkins

__04__/__25__/__08__
DATE

If you ever accepted an indecent proposal.

Expensive things get you off.

Your mouth opens like a cash register.

You go to the NBA draft to look for new talent.

You can make your own NBA dream team with the men you sleep with.

You subscribe to *Street & Smith's*.

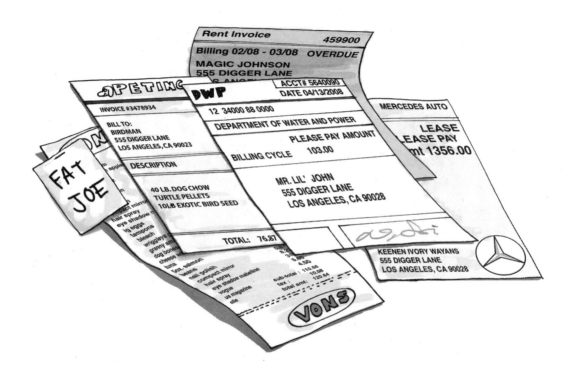

You have a different man to cover each bill.

You have more pictures of you with celebrities than of you with your kids.

You went to law school just to learn about pre-nup laws.

You work at McDonald's but you subscribe to *Forbes.*

You store more celebrity sperm than a sperm bank.

You live in a penthouse apartment and don't pay rent.

Your only job is to stay pretty.

You have two assistants and no job.

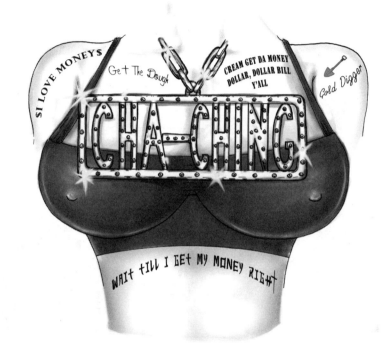

Your nickname is "Cha-Ching."

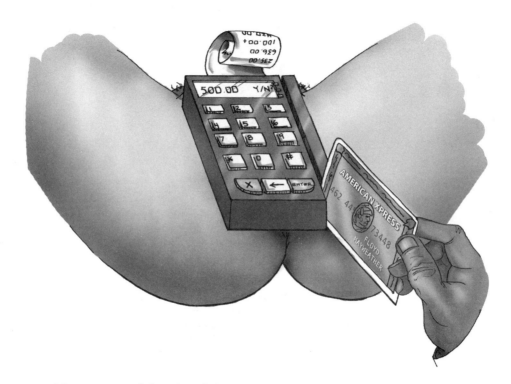

Your coochie doubles as a credit card terminal.

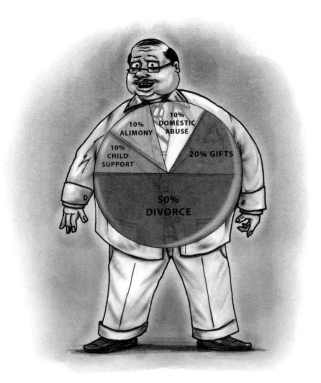

You look at your boyfriend as an investment.

You asked a rich guy to give you a car, breasts, braces, and child support on the first date.

You started a golddigger boot camp.

You pass up young handsome poor guy for fat ugly rich guy.

You wear name brands you can't pronounce.

You've ever eaten at an expensive sushi restaurant and referred to wasabi as "the green stuff."

Your boyfriend gives you jewelry and you get it appraised.

You went on strike with the NBA players to dispute the salary cap.

You have a statue at the hall of fame but never played a sport.

You have a better parking space at the stadium than the star player.

You were hired as a consultant for the movie *Almost Famous.*

You run a credit check on a guy before going on a date with him.

You wear a miner's hat to a club to look for a rich man.

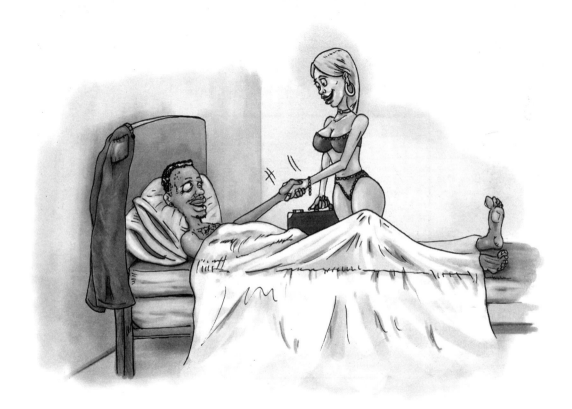

You refer to sleeping with a rich guy as "closing a deal."

Forbes
Biggest Financial Scandals

SCANDAL: Forbes saw a year of major scandals with the totals estimated in the billions. Forbes list the top three scandals that rocked the United States and beyond.

1. Shemeka Johnson
"Baby Daddy Scandal of 2008"

2. Bear-Stearns

3. Enron

PHOTO: SHEMEKA JOHNSON

Forbes. August 10, 2008

45

You cleared more bank accounts than Enron.

You spend more money than the man who makes it.

Your idea of a day at the office is shopping.

You spend your child support money on a personal chef for yourself while the children eat the big bag of Tyson chicken from Costco.

You have a guy order you Cristal even though it gives you gas.

You ask a guy what kind of car he drives before you ask him his name.

Your astrological sign is the dollar sign.

Your pubic hair is shaved in the shape of a dollar sign.

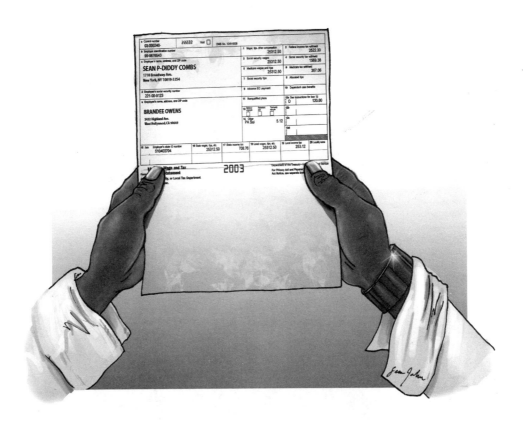

You send out W-2s at the end of all your relationships.

You have a subscription to *Forbes* and *The Robb Report*
but live in the projects.

You married a leprechaun just so you could get half his pot of gold.

You have a price list for things a girlfriend is supposed to do.

You pick up men at ATM machines instead of bars.

You get into clubs faster than someone famous.

You own more sports memorabilia than a licensed dealer.

You have a scrapbook full of hotel room keys.

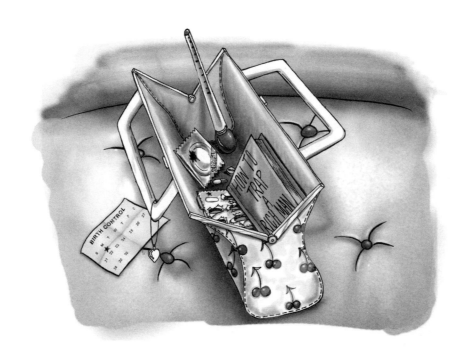

You carry a turkey baster in your purse.

You have a hotel suite named after you and you're not a president.

1998

PRESENT DAY

You sue a celebrity for an STD you already had.

People only know your name by the men you slept with.

You have more championship rings than Michael Jordan and never played a game.

NO

YES

You only tell famous men that you're allergic to latex condoms.

You travel with no luggage to see a guy but
come home with a whole new wardrobe.

Men you've dated had to file for bankruptcy after the first date.

Your name is in the credits of a rapper's album and you never worked on the project.

If you've ever dropped your family for a rich guy.

You slept with Ken Griffey, Sr. in the 60s and Ken Griffey, Jr. in the 90s.

You slept with Magic Johnson before and after
he announced that he has HIV.

You ever Googled a guy before you went on a date with him.

You know every rapper by his real name.

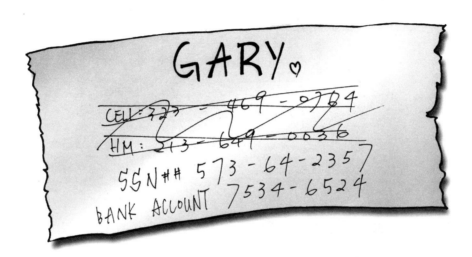

You ask for a guy's Social Security number instead of his phone number.

You teach your daughter how to catch a rich man.

You got pregnant just to collect child support.

You lie about your children's living expenses during your divorce to get more money to support your lifestyle.

Your first words were "Money" and "Dollar" instead of Mommy and Daddy.

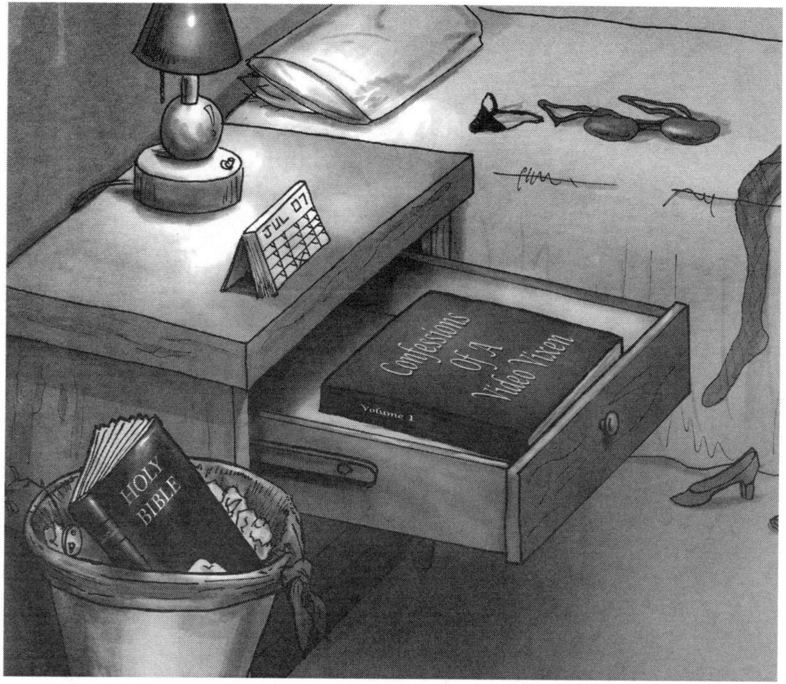
JUL 07
Confessions Of A Video Vixen
Volume 1
HOLY BIBLE

Confessions of a Video Vixen is on your bedside table instead of the Bible.

Your G-strings have pockets.

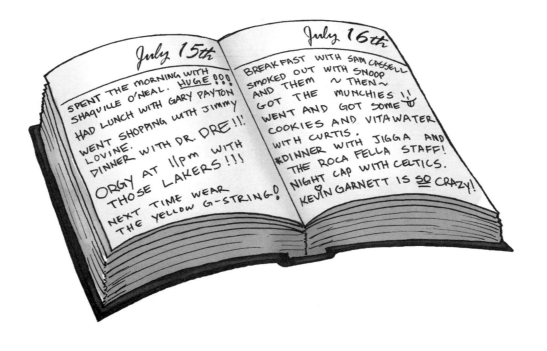

All your stories involve someone rich or famous.

You only know streets by the celebrities who live on them.

You've been to so many celebrity homes
you can start your own Star Maps business.

You act like you don't know who a celebrity is when you meet one.

Bill Gates

Oprah Winfrey

Keisha's Coochie

Forbes listed your vagina as one of the year's 100 wealthiest.

Your hands are shaped like money clips.

Treasure hunters use you as a gold detector.

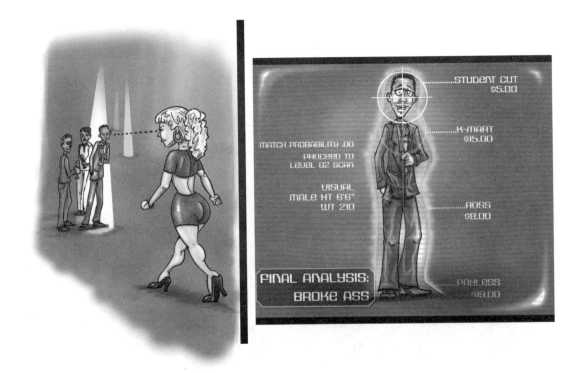

You can spot a broke man a mile away.

You count money instead of sheep.

WS ODC 2009